CM00662419

TALES ON BRITANNIA

Have a great read!

Tim O'Brien

TALES ON BRITANNIA

by

Tim J. O'Brien

Havens Edge Publishing

Tales on Britannia

Printed in the United Kingdom

First Printing, 2018

ISBN 978-1-9164511-0-0

Havens Edge Publishing,
Fife Scotland

My utmost gratitude and most sincere thanks go to Suzanne O'Brien - my daughter and Main Editor, who was at all times patient and wise beyond her years. Her endless effort, persistence and accuracy are now here to behold in this book. This work would not have read as it does without her insistence and dogged determination to just get it right.

Special thanks go to Elizabeth and Laura-Kate - my wife and daughter for their patience over the last year and their help in editing, correcting and rewriting of my initial scrawls. LK – thanks for the technical help!

Thanks to Sophie Lee for the incredible drawings that are all hand drawn- the originals of which she made in Indian Ink.

Many thanks go to Lucie for her time spent editing the near final copy of my book and to Derek and Oli for having the patience to read one of the earlier pre-edited manuscripts.

Also thank you to Ruth Armstrong for her patience and well done for being in the right place at the right time to do the photographs for the front and back covers.

Main Editor Suzanne O'Brien

Internal drawings courtesy of Sophie Lee

Email sophielee.illustration@gmail.com

Front and back cover photographs courtesy of
Ruth Armstrong

Email ruth@rutharmstrongphotography.com
or Facebook @rutharmstrongphotography

Contact Tim on Facebook @TimJOBrienVA

CONTENTS

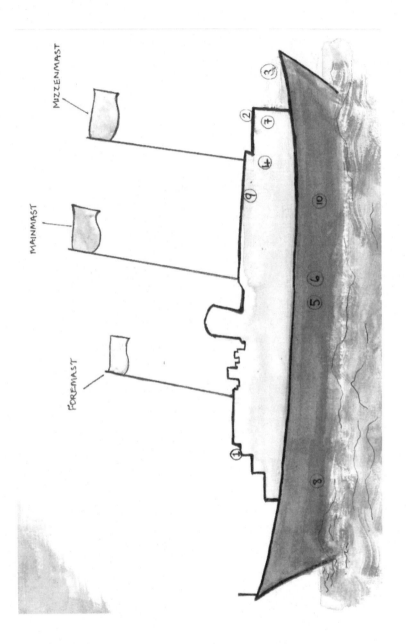

MIZZENMAST

MAINMAST

FOREMAST

2

1. Royal Bridge
2. Verandah Deck
3. Quarter Deck
4. Grand Staircase
5. Boiler Room

6. Engine Room
7. Drawing Room
8. Crews Accommodation
9. Royal Apartments
10. Household Staff Accommodation

FOREWORD

I am currently a Tour Guide and Visitor Assistant on The Royal Yacht *Britannia* and have been for the past two years.

I decided to embark on a mission to put down in words some Royal Yacht *Britannia* memories, which I have researched and discovered through word of mouth from fellow Visitor Assistants (both past and present), former Yotties (crew members), Maintenance Staff and other Shipboard Personnel. I have come to love retelling these anecdotes and stories to our visitors, my family and friends.

My ramblings have come from research into the history of Royal Yachts going back nearly 400 years. It would be impossible to cover everything, so I have picked out the aspects that I find most interesting. Some of the information you can hear on the tour of *Britannia*, but most is new or additional material.

Some of my anecdotes are drawn from my real-life experiences, having spent 4 years as a Merchant Navy Deck Cadet sailing with Shell Tankers UK Ltd, nearly 8 years in the Royal Air Force as an Aircraft Electronics Technician (Harriers and Tornado F3), and over 20 years in the Police. I retired from the Police in 2013 and found my current job on board *Britannia* whilst browsing the internet. My job on the *Britannia* is more of a vocation for me – I love it and hope to do so for many more years.

As a result of my various careers I have had the greatest pleasure, privilege and honour to meet Prince Charles, Princess Diana and Princess Anne.

This book is intended as a mini reference guide and I do hope that those who read it are able to imagine the circumstances involved and hopefully on occasions have a little laugh. Absolutely no offence is meant towards those involved in my anecdotes - in fact the opposite - I just want to tell as many people as possible about this fantastic piece of history. Please enjoy this book.

INTRODUCTION

A yacht is a sailing vessel for racing with either steam, sail, or other motive power. It can be a vessel for pleasure trips and cruising, or a State vessel for the use of The Royal Family or Government Officials.

Britannia was and continues to be one of the most iconic sights in the world. No matter where she travelled she was instantly recognised as The Royal Yacht of Her Majesty The Queen. She sailed 1,087,623 nautical miles - which is the equivalent of one circumnavigation of the world for each of her 44 years of service. She completed 85 State visits, visited 135 countries and made nearly 700 visits worldwide.

When Her Majesty was on board she would take an entourage in the region of 50 staff, including: a Physician, Chefs, Ladies in Waiting and Stewards, to name just a few. She would also be accompanied by a contingent of Royal Marines Band bandsmen, who numbered between 20-30, (In addition to providing musical entertainment they would take care of security for The Royal Family). Latterly, there were 220 Crew and 20 Officers - which included 1 Admiral.

BRITANNIA FACTS AND FIGURES

Cost to build	£2,098,000
Royal Apartment's cost	

- Internal decoration   £76,000
- Carpeting   £9,000

Length overall	412' 3" or 125.65m.
Length at the waterline	380' or 115.82m.
Length between perpendiculars	360' or 109.73m.
Maximum beam	55' or 16.76m.
Depth amidships	45' or 13.72m.
Draft	15'7 $^1/_2$" or 4.8m.
Gross tonnage	5769 tons.
Displacement	4715 tons.

Propellers - Four bladed propellers made of manganese bronze.

- Diameter   10'3" or 3.12m.
- Pitch   9' or 2.74m.

Foremast height	133' or 40.54m with a rake of 1 $^5/_8$" per ft. (Lord High Admiral flag).
Mainmast height	139'3" or 42.44m with a rake (slope) of 1 $^3/_4$" per ft. (Royal Standard or most senior person on board).
Mizzenmast height	118'10" or 36.22m with a rake of 1 $^7/_8$" per ft. (Union flag).

Between deck heights - 8' in general around the Yacht and 10' high in the State Rooms.

Bulwark height at bow - 6' and 3'6" elsewhere.

Engines - two high pressure and two low pressure Parsons Marine Steam Turbines developing 12,000 shaft horse power, for a maximum speed of 22 $^1/_2$ knots.

Boilers - two main boilers and one auxiliary boiler (for use in harbour), all manufactured by Foster Wheeler.

Standby Generator - Paxman six-cylinder diesel engine formerly from the submarine HMS Vampire (affectionately known as Chitty Chitty Bang Bang).

Fuel consumption - 21.5 tons at peak load.

Range - 2196 nautical miles at 20 knots and 2553 nautical miles at 18 knots.

Fuel capacity - 330 tons which could be increased to 490 tons.

Fresh water capacity - 120 tons which could be increased to 195 tons.

3 x 60cwt (3 ton) Admiralty Pattern Stockless Bower Anchors with 8-10 shackles of 1 $^7/_8$" forged steel stud link cable.

1 x 20cwt (1 ton) Admiralty Pattern Stockless Cast Head Stream Anchor.

1 x 300 lb Danforth Kedge Anchor.

Forecastle Electrical Capstan - 20 tons at 25 ft per minute.

Aft Quarter Deck Electrical Capstan - 5 tons at 25 ft per minute.

The 24-carat gold band painted around the hull of the Yacht cost £90 for paint and £150 for labour in 1953.

A BRIEF HISTORY OF ROYAL YACHTS

There have been a total of 83 Royal Yachts up until *Britannia,* some more famous than others.

The first Royal Yacht following the Restoration of the Monarchy was HMY *Mary* of 1660, which was Charles II's yacht. She weighed less than 100 tons, was 50 ft long and carried 6 three-pound cannons. In 1675 she was shipwrecked off Anglesey in very poor visibility.

On 1st September 1842, Queen Victoria visited Granton, Edinburgh, in the *Royal George* (a sail powered Yacht), where she was greeted by The Duke of Buccleuch and Prime Minister Sir Robert Peel. This was Victoria's first of many visits to Scotland - *I think it is fair to say she fell in love with the country.* On her journey to Edinburgh, the Yacht was overtaken by numerous steam driven vessels, needless to say, Victoria was not amused. Unsurprisingly, it was not long after this that she acquired the *Victoria and Albert I* and later, the *Victoria and Albert II,* which were both paddle driven steamers that were not reliant on wind for their power.

The *Alberta* (a passage boat to the *Victoria and Albert II*), came to be Victoria's favourite Royal Yacht. She used her regularly to travel between her beloved Osbourne House on the Isle of Wight and the UK mainland.

In Oban, on the West Coast of Scotland, there is an old photograph on a hotel wall which depicts a ship that appears to have been cut in half. The stricken vessel was in fact the *Mistletoe.* She had been struck amidships by Her Majesty's Yacht *Alberta,* near to the Isle of Wight in 1875. Queen Victoria was on board at that time, as was Prince Ernest.

At a subsequent Board of Inquiry, the *Alberta's* Staff Captain was reprimanded, and reparations were paid to the victims' families.

The Victoria and Albert III (the Royal Yacht prior to *Britannia*), was floated from her dry dock in 1899, and immediately took a list of 8 degrees to port. Queen Victoria heard about this and swore never to sail on her. It was thought that the ships architects had obtained plans for a similar yacht built in Russia, but there appeared to have been some ambiguity over whether the plans were in imperial or metric measurements! Although another perhaps more likely explanation is that the problem was to do with additional weight used in construction - particularly extra soundproofing around the Royal Apartments. She was 380 ft long, weighed approximately 4,700 tons and cost around half a million pounds to construct. She saw service from 1901-1939 and had an ignominious end as an accommodation hulk in Portsmouth, until she was eventually scrapped in 1954. However, there was good news as quite a lot of priceless maritime artefacts were saved from her, and have eventually found their way onto the Royal Yacht *Britannia*. For example, the Yacht's magnetic compass binnacle (see pages 34-36) which originally came from the *Royal George* of 1817.

There have been 7 ships named *Britannia* in total. The penultimate one was launched in 1893, which measured 121 ft long and weighed 221 tons. She was a gaff-rigged racing cutter owned by King Edward VII and King George V. This vessel was scuttled at Winchelsea near to St Catherine's Point Lighthouse off the Isle of Wight, by the crew of *HMS Amazon* in 1936. This was a direct result of the deceased Kings' wishes. Luckily her ship's wheel was saved and used in the Wheelhouse of the current *Britannia*. It is now on display in the *Britannia* Visitor Centre in Leith.

From 1939 there was no Royal Yacht, although discussions and detailed proposals were on the table in 1938. However, the Munich Crisis and World War II saw an end to these deliberations.

Both the main political parties believed such a project post-war would be good for the morale of the country and give a boost to at least one shipyard. Therefore, the Government resurrected the plans in mid-1951, and various shipyards were approached and asked to submit proposals. John Brown & Company Ltd. of Clydebank emerged as the preferred bidder. As one of the biggest shipbuilders in the world, they built hundreds of ships including *HMS Hood* (sunk in the North Atlantic by the *Bismarck*), *RMS Queen Mary* (now moored as a visitor attraction at Long Beach, California), *RMS Queen Elizabeth* (sank after a fire in Hong Kong harbour and now lies under reclaimed land), and *RMS Lusitania* (torpedoed and sunk by a submarine in WW1), to name a few. One of the main reasons they were the preferred bidders was that they had recently built two cross channel ferries (the *Arnhem* and the *Amsterdam*), and the plans for these vessels were very similar to the requirements for the new Royal Yacht. In addition, they were ready to commence manufacture immediately. The estimated cost at this time was £3 million.

King George VI had been in poor health and it was thought that a new Royal Yacht might help to speed up his recovery. On 4th February 1952, the order was placed to commence the planning and the build - she was job number 691 for John Brown's. Unfortunately, two days later The King died of lung cancer at the age of 56, and his daughter Elizabeth became The Queen.

Commencing the build on 16th June 1952, *Britannia's* keel was laid. She was launched by The Queen on 16th April 1953. Her name had been kept a closely guarded secret, which led to one of the most iconic moments when her majesty revealed the name,

"I name this ship Britannia, I wish success to her and to all who sail in her".

She then released the bottle of empire wine which smashed against *Britannia's* side, to the rapturous applause and cheers from the crowds who had gathered for this momentous event. It was also a particularly special moment as this was the first yacht Her Majesty had launched since her accession to the throne.

She was commissioned into the Royal Navy on 11th January 1954, following extensive trials.

CAPTAIN DALGLISH

Captain James Stephen Dalglish was *Britannia's* Commanding Officer whilst she was being fitted out at John Brown's shipyard, and in her run up to being commissioned. The Captain sent weekly newsletters to Vice Admiral Able-Smith (who at the time was on the post-Coronation tour of Australia and New Zealand, with Her Majesty and Prince Philip on the *SS Gothic*), detailing the preparations for commissioning.

Dalglish reported that a pint of beer cost 9d (that is 9 old pennies which equates to approximately 4 new pence), per pint - *which was a cheap pint!* As on all Royal Navy ships, the beer was the standard CSB (Courage Sparkling Bitter). This special brew was only available to the Royal Navy.

On other occasions, he reported incidents such as: rain water leaks in the Charthouse, the sewage tank overflowed due to an item left by the manufacturer, and the ship's steam sirens jammed - *which would have been quite annoying!* One particularly embarrassing incident occurred when one of *Britannia's* small motor boat tenders rammed the Yacht head-on, although it only caused minor damage.

One major defect that he highlighted was that the ship's paint (the paint colour of *Britannia* was chosen by The Queen and was in fact the same colour as her Dragon Class racing yacht *Bluebottle*), had apparently been applied in frosty conditions and as a result it peeled to such an extent that she had to be fully stripped back to bare metal and repainted.

There were other problems with the welding on the funnels. Just like with any new build there were numerous snags most of which were remedied swiftly by the crew or John Brown's staff.

He also commented that Britannia did not handle like a destroyer. On approach to a mooring buoy she failed to slow down quickly enough, and the buoy scraped all the way up the ship's starboard side and emerged from the stern. A month or so after this incident, when members of the crew decided to enjoy the warm waters of the Mediterranean, they observed damage to one of the propellers.

Perhaps this had been caused by the same incident.

THE YACHT

THE BRIDGE

When at sea the Bridge was manned by the Officer of the Watch, a Lookout and a Signalman. When entering port or busy seas (such as the English Channel), others including the Admiral would be there. During her 44 years in commission only the Admiral was entitled to sit on the chair located on the Bridge. Nowadays visitors often take the opportunity to snap a photo of themselves in the hot seat - *unaware of the wrath that could have been incurred from the Admiral if he was still in charge!*

The Bridge and funnel are manufactured in aluminium to keep weight low, thus making the ship more stable. Hence, the Bridge is quite vulnerable to damage, which is one of the reasons why the ship's wheel and engine telegraphs are located below the Bridge in the Wheelhouse. Today the Wheelhouse is preserved in the form of a display in the Visitor Centre entrance to *Britannia*.

The current Admiralty Chart on the Bridge plots the course taken by *Britannia* as she navigated the Firth of Forth in May 1998, and into Leith – her final home port. She was towed by a tug as her engines had been decommissioned in Portsmouth.

Located in the Chartroom and on the Bridge there are: radios, charts, sonar, satellite navigation systems, almanacs, chronometers, a Decca navigator, a sextant and a facsimile machine which received weather reports. Even in the 1980s, only a couple of weather charts were received each day, and as a result of this, they were always eagerly awaited by all the ship's staff and no doubt The Royal Family as well.

The main gyro compass equipment is situated below deck just forward of the Generator Room, in a position of minimal vibration and maximum stability. The gyro compass binnacle on the Bridge houses one of the seven gyro compass repeaters. The other six are located as follows: one on each Bridge wing, one in the Royal Bridge, one in the Wheelhouse, one on the Verandah Deck and the last in the Emergency Steering Compartment.

As with all ships, the *Britannia* has a magnetic compass (on ships these days it is generally used as a backup for use in emergencies), housed within a wooden binnacle in the centre of the Bridge. The one that is currently on board came from the *Victoria and Albert III*. The small iron balls (which were patented by Lord Kelvin in the 1880s), situated on either side of it can be adjusted to offset the magnetic influence of the ship. The iron bar in front of the compass is called a 'flinders bar' and has a similar effect to the balls.

Following a refit to a ship, the crew will carry out manoeuvres known as Swinging the Compass. This manoeuvre requires the ship to be taken into an area of open water free of any other traffic. This gives the ship and crew a clear area to move the ship through the eight main compass points (north, north-east, east, south-east, south, south-west, west and north-west). The ship's magnetic compass headings are compared with the actual magnetic heading and any inconsistencies are known as the deviation. This deviation is compensated for by use of the balls and other magnets and a deviation card is produced.

Ahead of the Falklands War, all Merchant ships that were commandeered for duty were fitted with satellite communications and navigating systems. On their return (once they had been discharged from their war duties), this equipment was removed. *Britannia* was in line for some of this equipment, but the supplier decided that *Britannia* should be given new equipment which was subsequently fitted in 1982.

ADMIRAL'S ACCOMMODATION

The Admiral's Quarters consist of a living room, dining room (separated by a curtain), a bedroom and a separate bathroom – he was the only member of the crew to have his own bath. Much of the furniture in his quarters is from the early 1900s and originally came from the previous Royal Yacht, the *Victoria and Albert III*.

The oil painting above the Admiral's desk depicts the Royal Yacht *Alberta* being followed by *Victoria and Albert II*. The colours (mainmast flag), flying on *Alberta*, are those of Queen Victoria and are at half-mast showing that she had died and is on-board being transported from the Isle of Wight to the mainland for burial. She was being escorted by her eldest son the new King, King Edward VII, whose colours are flying on *Victoria and Albert II*.
The clouds in the background appear to show the crowned head of a figure - perhaps the artist is trying to show that Victoria is still there.

The corridor to the rear of the Admiral's Quarters incorporates the Senior Officers' cabins and is known as the Whispering Corridor. Just down the stairs from there is the Officer's Wardroom and Anteroom. *I can only assume that after an evening of merriment and possibly the odd drink, the Officers had the sense to whisper as they returned to their cabins, so as not to incur the wrath of their boss - the Admiral.* In addition, any member of the crew who had occasion to be there, also knew that he had to be very quiet.

The oil painting currently in the Whispering Corridor above the stairway, depicts HMS *Britannia* (a three decked hundred-gun, ship of the line – which means she would engage enemy vessels side on, allowing the full weight of her cannons to come to bare on the other vessel in what is termed a 'broadside'), as she enters Grand Harbour, Valetta, Malta circa 1810. This ship was involved in Admiral Nelson's famous victory over the combined French and Spanish Fleet, at the Battle of Trafalgar on 21st October 1805.

19

GARAGE

The Rolls Royce Phantom V (see page 42)(6.23 litre, V8, 4-speed automatic gearbox), located in the garage, fitted perfectly but only after the bumpers had been removed. A Rolls Royce engineer generally travelled on board when the car was required, to fix any problems and of course to fix and remove the bumpers.

When The Royal Family went on their annual Western Isles Cruise off the coast of Scotland, they often replaced the Rolls Royce with a Land Rover, as this vehicle was more suited to the terrain. The first time the Land Rover was taken ashore, two of the ships' Jolly boats (small motor boats), were strapped together and the Land Rover precariously placed on top. The following year a floating pontoon was used, which could easily be towed with the Land Rover strapped to it. This proved much more suitable and stable.

ROYAL BARGE

The current Royal Barge came to Britannia in 1964 (as a replacement for the previous one which had been used on the *Victoria and Albert III*), and was stowed on davits directly above the Rolls Royce. It was used to convey The Royal Family backwards and forwards to *Britannia* when she was at anchor. The Barge was recommissioned for The Queen's Diamond Jubilee celebrations in 2012. Some ex-members of the crew, with assistance from current maintenance staff, made tireless efforts in their spare time and holidays to get her up to an impeccable standard - allowing her to pass stringent tests on the Thames. These tests involved, checking her reliability, watertight integrity and her engine's performance. She then returned to Leith where she was painted and polished prior to her duty of conveying Her Majesty and Prince Philip from Cadogan Pier, Chelsea, to the *Spirit of Chartwell* for the cruise on the Thames, with hundreds of small boats in the flotilla. Two of Britannias' fast motor launches (FMLs) also accompanied the Barge - just as they would have done when *Britannia* was in commission.

VERANDAH DECK

The Royal Family would use the Verandah Deck for recreational activities such as deck tennis or quoits. Often a portable swimming pool was erected, and the children would play on a water slide that was constructed on the stairs to the deck.

The compass binnacle (see pages 34 to 36), which is currently on the Verandah Deck is a replica of the two which were originally made for the *Royal George* (the Royal Yacht of 1817). One of these two original binnacles is in the *Britannia* Visitor Centre (this was fitted to *Britannia* during her commission), whilst the other is at the National Maritime Museum in Greenwich. They were each constructed from a solid piece of mahogany and were decorated in 24-carat gold leaf, with painted fish and octopus. They both originally housed a magnetic compass, but the replica fitted to *Britannia* today houses a gyro compass repeater.

The Verandah Deck could have been used as an emergency conning position (should the Bridge have been out of action), as behind the wooden doors located near to the binnacle, is a magnetic compass along with telephones linking to the Bridge, Wheelhouse, Engine Room and Emergency Steering Compartment.

The ship's bell (see page 37 and 38), that was originally on the Verandah Deck was of bronze construction, with a chrome finish and was cast by Tommy Swift who worked for TM Utley in St Helens. The bell was rung on ceremonial occasions and at midnight on New Year's Day - 8 times for the Old Year and 8 times for the New Year. Over the 44 years the bell was so highly polished to keep up with the high standards set on board that some of the inscription - "PRESENTED TO HER

MAJESTY THE QUEEN BY THE CORPORATION OF TRINITY HOUSE 21st OCTOBER 1953" - had become so faint that it was almost illegible. It was originally gifted to Her Majesty by the Senior Brethren of Trinity House and was returned to Trinity House, Tower Hill London (Princess Anne is a Patron of Trinity House), when Britannia was decommissioned. The bell was taken to Whitechapel Bell Foundry (which is the company that cast both the Liberty Bell and Big Ben), for the etching to be repaired. The etching was done in such a way for it to look as authentic as possible.

A source at the foundry tells me that the bell was kept under the Managing Director's desk for safekeeping whilst in his possession.

The bell, that is currently situated on the Verandah Deck is of similar construction and was originally fitted to the front of *Britannia* during her service. It was used for christenings of some of the crew's children.

The Coat of Arms (see pages 37 and 39) directly above the bell came from the *Victoria and Albert II*

SUN LOUNGE

The Sun Lounge was The Queen's favourite room, where she would regularly have breakfast and afternoon tea.

Within the Sun Lounge it was customary to display an Admiralty Chart of the area that *Britannia* was sailing in, to allow The Royal Family to see where they were and where they were going. The one currently displayed shows Hong Kong, as this was *Britannia's* last major duty, when Hong Kong was handed back to China after Britain's 99-year lease ended in 1997.

The rum tub in the Sun Lounge was usually kept in the crew's accommodation below decks. Prior to 1970, the crew were issued a daily rum allowance. This was in the form of what is known as grog, which is a mixture of water and rum in the ratio of 3:1. This had to be checked by an Officer to make sure that it was the correct mixture - *a job I am sure that he enjoyed.* The ration (which amounted to half a pint), had to be drunk when issued and not stored for a party - *which was perhaps a great disappointment for the crew!*

During her reign, Queen Victoria once tasted the grog and is said to have commented that it was a little weak for her liking.

ROYAL APARTMENTS

Britannia had bad vibrations, particularly in The Queens' apartments at speeds between 12 and 18 knots. To ensure Her Majesty and the rest of the passengers on board had a comfortable sail, the Admiral would ensure that *Britannia* maintained speeds above 18 knots during the day, and at night time would sail at speeds below 12 knots. Measures were taken to try to stop the vibrations, for example, more strengthening around The Queens' quarters and 5 bladed propellers were tried, however these remedies proved ineffective.

The Queen's wardrobe room is located just forward of the main guest suite. Her majesty travelled with anywhere between 2 and 5 tonnes of luggage. It housed (and in fact still does house), a rather imposing looking safe for The Queen's jewellery. The Dukes dressing room and a small pantry are also located nearby.

Below the State Rooms there were 16 guest rooms, 12 of which were suites with sitting rooms and bathrooms. (other members of the Royal used these suites when on board). These rooms were fitted out to a standard similar to that of a first-class cabin on a cruise ship.

There was always a good show of flowers around the Royal Apartments. When in home waters, these flowers were obtained from Windsor Castle, but otherwise they were sourced locally. To keep the flowers fresh they were stored in one of *Britannia's* cold rooms. Today the fantastic fresh flower displays are sourced locally in Edinburgh.

Amongst the many photographs of The Royal Family and other memorabilia on board *Britannia* today, there are three photographs which are particularly worth mentioning :

- The first is located in the Sun Lounge. It shows The Royal Family alongside a small speedboat, which was gifted to Her Majesty by Cunard after she launched the *Queen Elizabeth II* in September 1967.
- The second, which is adjacent to The Queen's bedroom, depicts four Kings: - Edward VII, George V, Edward VIII and George VI. It was taken on board the *Victoria and Albert III* by Edward VII's wife, Alexandra, in 1905.
- The third, which is near to the main guest room, shows members of The Queen's immediate family all wearing their respective service uniforms. Her Majesty is wearing a dark cloak which is the uniform of the Lord High Admiral (a title which she subsequently bestowed on The Duke of Edinburgh for his 90th birthday). Prince Philip, Prince Charles, Princess Anne and Prince Andrew are in their respective Royal Navy uniforms. What is noteworthy about this picture is that it includes Prince Edward who is wearing his Royal Marines uniform, as he was only in that service for a matter of months and resigned in January 1987. Therefore, to see all The Royal Family together in their uniforms, makes this a particularly special photograph.

WARDROOM ANTEROOM

Near the entrance to the Officer's Anteroom there is a wooden tally board which was used to confirm who was on board at the time. At first glance it isn't noticeable, but on closer inspection there is a spelling error of the word Royal, having been spelt as 'Royay'.

Also on display is an original oil painting of the 'Raid on St Nazaire' by John Worsley, dated 1982 – commemorating 40 years since the raid in 1942.

There are numerous fantastic pieces of history in the Officer's Anteroom, such as:

- Pride of place over the fireplace are photographs of Her Majesty The Queen and Prince Philip taken in 1954, near the time of *Britannia's* commissioning.
- The blue and white plate located on one of the walls is from number 5 Mess on board the *Victoria and Albert III*.
- The photograph of Queen Victoria with her signature, shows her looking straight across the room, perhaps poignantly, at her eldest son Edward VII.
- A silver sailing ship within the display cabinet behind the bar is the top of a salt cellar. It was gifted to the Officers of the *Victoria and Albert III* by the Russian Queen, Queen Alexandra in 1906 (who was a member of the ill-fated Romanov dynasty). The ship supposedly came from the table of The Tsar Nicholas II.
- A piece of limited edition Gibraltar crystal is situated behind the bar which commemorates *Britannia's* last visit to Gibraltar prior to her decommissioning.
  (Gibraltar was *Britannia's* last overseas port of call).

Personally, what I believe to be one of the best exhibits on board is Admiral Lord Nelson's uniform button. It was presented to the Officers of the Wardroom in 1925, by the 5th Duke of Bronte - the 1st Duke of Bronte being Admiral Lord Nelson himself. Nelson was made The Duke of Bronte by King Ferdinand of Italy following a conflict in Naples, where Nelson had performed a great service to the King. In addition to the title, Nelson was gifted a parcel of land on Sicily, near to Mount Etna, which included a Monastery and Maniace Castle.

I was recounting this particular story about Nelson's button to a visitor on Britannia and he was suitably impressed. However, he mentioned that he had been at the National Maritime Museum in Greenwich the week before, where he had seen Nelson's full uniform. Quick as a flash I said, "Yes but I think that you will find that it is missing a button!"

Next to Nelson's button there is a copy of an oil painting by Clarkson Stanfield, depicting the badly damaged *HMS Victory (Nelson's flagship)*, heading into Gibraltar, just after the battle of Trafalgar in October 1805.

Nelson had received a fatal bullet wound from a French sharpshooter who was on the French ship *Redoubtable*. The *Victory* was towed to Gibraltar by HMS Neptune, she then made her own way under jury-rig into Rosia Bay, Gibraltar. Once the *Victory* was repaired, Nelson's body was taken to Britain for burial in St Paul's Cathedral, London. This was apparently against his wishes as he had wanted to be buried at Burnham Thorpe, Norfolk, alongside his parents.

There are stories which tell of his body being placed in a barrel of rum or brandy, and that when his body was uncased, some of the liquid contents had been syphoned off and drunk - supposedly by the ship's crew. Apparently, this is where the term 'Nelson's Blood' (as Rum is known in the Royal Navy), comes from.

On a lighter note, the Officers were gifted a wombat cuddly toy from one of The Queen's Ladies-in-Waiting, on the condition that they were to look after it properly – *of course they didn't!* In fact, they devised a game known as 'Wombat Tennis', where the toy was hurled into a ceiling fan and then knocked around the room. Needless to say, he spent most of his time in the Yacht's Sick Bay undergoing repairs.

WARDROOM

The Wardroom is the Officer's Dining Room. Breakfast and lunch were informal occasions, whilst dinner was more formal. This was when the Officers would wear the traditional Red Sea Rig, consisting of patent leather shoes, black trousers with black cummerbund and a white shirt. When toasting Her Majesty in the Wardroom, the toast was taken standing as an extra mark of respect. This is not the case on other Royal Navy ships, (no doubt to stop the Officers from banging their heads), as it is said, when King Charles II was replying to a toast aboard the *Royal Charles*, he stood up and bumped his head on the deckhead (ceiling)!

The dining chair legs in the Wardroom were cut to different levels to overcome the ships 9-inch camber, allowing the Officers to sit at the correct angle.

Carrying on the earlier Nelson theme, there is a telescope within this room mounted on a plinth made from timbers obtained from his flagship *HMS Victory*.

One piece of silverware worth special mention is a silver Pegasus bowl (with handles in the form of winged horses), which depicts four previous Royal Yachts. There are also two silver Cromwellian urns, each dated 1909 (gifted by a previous Royal Yacht Admiral, Admiral Keppel), and a gin pennant. When a member of the Wardroom was celebrating a special occasion (perhaps a birthday or an anniversary), he would raise the pennant indicating that he was buying the drinks.

STATE DINING ROOM

State Banquets were held in the State Dining Room and seated up to 56 guests. There was a top table at which Her Majesty would sit with her back to the sword (a gift from the Swedish Navy in 1956), on the forward bulkhead. Other members of The Royal Family and the guest of honour would be seated alongside her. The tables on the port and starboard sides of the room seated other guests, and were headed by the Head of The Queen's Household and the Admiral.

On these occasions, all three Galleys i.e. Royal Galley, Officer's Galley and Crew's Galley, would work together to produce the banquet.

The original dining room table (which is now at Frogmore House, in the grounds of Windsor Castle), had a very interesting modification designed by the Admiral Earl of Mountbatten. He was not particularly happy with lights being plugged in with unsightly wires lying about, so he designed an electric channel which ran the length of the table. This allowed the lights to be plugged in wherever they were needed – *this was a very innovative modification.*

Ordinary dinners were also taken in this room and the Admiral would regularly eat with Her Majesty along with other Officers.

Just underneath the Grand Staircase (see page 40), between the State Dining Room and the State Anteroom are The Queen and Duke's studies. In a manner similar to that of their bedrooms, they had lights outside the entrance doors to indicate when visitors should enter or not, and they also had telephones so that they could contact each other should they so desire.

The ornamental leaf decorations in this area are of hand beaten copper, whilst the Grand Staircase is manufactured from anodised aluminium. They have the appearance of gold creating an impressive sense of grandeur.

Near to The Queen and Dukes' Studies, there are several hand drawn fleet review charts. Over the years, fleet reviews have been carried out periodically by members of The Royal Family to commemorate various events, in particular:

- The 1935 Silver Jubilee of George V and the 1937 Coronation Review of George VI - both of which were carried out on the *Victoria and Albert III*.
- The 1953 Queen's Coronation Review was carried out on *HMS Surprise* (an anti-aircraft frigate). There were 14 miles of ships from both the British fleets and those of Foreign and Commonwealth powers.
- The 1977 Silver Jubilee Review carried out on *Britannia*.

It was always said that *Britannia* was like Her Majesty's second home. Supposedly after a full day of engagements - on her return to *Britannia* - the double wooden doors would be closed behind her, and Her Majesty would often sit on the Grand Staircase, kick off her shoes and let out a long relaxing sigh - as if to say - I can now relax because I am home.

STATE ANTEROOM

The State Anteroom was often used for pre and post dinner drinks.

There is a large display cabinet in the corner of the Anteroom, which once stood in Buckingham Palace and was also on board the *Victoria and Albert III*. When *Britannia* was decommissioned, each member of The Royal Family was allowed one article as a keepsake, as a small reminder of their time on board. Prince Charles asked for the cabinet, but he was told that he had already had his choice and was not allowed a second - *I wonder who had the unenviable task of informing him!*

Coins from under the masts of *Victoria and Albert III* used to be housed in this cabinet, these consisted of 9 coins in total; 3 gold, 3 silver and 3 copper. They are all now located at Frogmore House.

Under each of the three masts on *Britannia* there is a Commonwealth coin and shilling housed in a metal box (as her masts are hollow), to ward off evil spirits. This tradition is thought to date back to Roman times where coins were placed as payment to the underworld should the ship be shipwrecked. In times gone by, the weight of the wooden masts often squashed the coins placed there.

STATE DRAWING ROOM

The State Drawing Room was a spacious and elegant place for The Royal Family to relax in or to entertain guests. A Welmar baby grand piano stands in the room and was played by many famous and notable people including Princess Diana and Sir Noel Coward. This Piano cost a grand total of £350 - *I cannot begin to imagine how much it is worth today!*

If you are wondering if there was a television in the State Drawing Room – then yes, there was. It was in a wooden cabinet made during one of Britannia's refits, and is currently located at the aft end starboard side of the room. No doubt there was also a video player in there as well.

PETTY OFFICERS' MESS

In the corner of the Petty Officers' Mess in a glass display cabinet, is a copy of *The Times* dated 1805. It tells the story of the Battle of Trafalgar and has quotes from Vice-Admiral Collingwood (Nelson's second-in-command), which vividly describes the battle.

Near to this, is one of *Britannia's* old steam activated, chrome plated, ship's whistles, which has cleverly been made into a bar stool. The matching stool is now owned by a Yottie from the Isle of Wight. When *Britannia* was decommissioned, a lot of paraphernalia was sold off by auction to the Yotties in aid of charity - *he paid £30 for the stool.*

SICK BAY

The Sick Bay was manned by a Surgeon Commander and two Petty Officers, one of whom was a theatre assistant and the other a physiotherapist. The crew would attend the Sick Bay for any injuries and illnesses. However, on more than one occasion this area was used to treat foreign nationals for various complaints and injuries from appendicitis to severe burns.

LAUNDRY

The ship's crew ran the laundry (usually civilian's ran the laundry on Royal Navy ships), and often worked here for up to four months at a time with a Petty Officer in charge. It was a non-profit making venture at 6p per shirt and 22p per white tropical uniform. *I am told by one of the Yotties that if there was any extra money after their time spent in the laundry, then it was put towards a "beer call" for the crew - a little reward for their hard work.*

ENGINE ROOM

The Engine Room was always kept immaculately clean. Prior to entering, those visiting were expected to wipe their feet on a strategically placed door mat – thus highlighting the lengths that were taken to keep it as clean as possible. The brasses were highly polished, and it was just as clean as all other areas on *Britannia*. There were generally eight crew members working from here, who might also be called upon to fix, repair and maintain other equipment around the Yacht. One thing that did help with its cleanliness was the fact that it was steam driven, and this is inherently clean especially when compared to a diesel engine.

When *Britannia* was in Tampa on the west coast of Florida, the Commander of the Allied Forces during Operation Desert Storm in the 1991 Gulf War, General Norman Schwarzkopf or 'Stormin' Norman' as he was known (*my boss when I was there with a squadron of Royal Air Force, Tornado F3 fighters from 43 Squadron*), came on board. He was dumbfounded by the complexity and cleanliness of the Engine Room. (Later, he was awarded an honorary Knighthood).

Royal Garter

Compass Binnacle

Compass

Decorative Fish from
Compass Binnacle

Coat of Arms and
Ship's Bell

Ship's Bell

Coat of Arms from the
Victoria and Albert II

Grand Staircase

Toronto - 1991

41

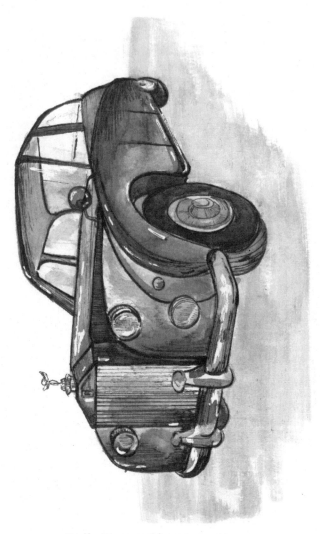

Rolls Royce Phantom V

BRITANNIA - 44 YEARS OF SERVICE TO THE QUEEN AND COUNTRY

1954

As *Britannia* was sailing underneath the Forth Rail Bridge on her way towards the North Sea, a penny landed on her Bridge. In those days, it was a tradition for train passengers crossing the Bridge to throw a penny out of the window of the train carriage for good luck. *I like to think that this contributed to Britannia's luck over her superb 44 years of service to The Queen and Country.*

On 14th April 1954, *Britannia* commenced her first Royal duty, which was to convey Prince Charles and Princess Anne from Portsmouth via Malta (her first foreign port of call), to Tobruk in Libya. As *Britannia* sailed out of Portsmouth, three members of The Queen's Household staff were observed on deck not wearing hats. As a result of their informal appearance, *Britannia* received a strongly worded message from the Commander in Chief of Portsmouth – *perhaps not the best start for these royal crew members.* When they reached Libya, they met Her Majesty The Queen and The Duke of Edinburgh, who were completing their Coronation tour of Australia and New Zealand in the *SS Gothic*.

Shortly after leaving Tobruk, *Britannia* met the Mediterranean fleet, which was under the command of Admiral Earl Mountbatten of Burma, which steamed past *Britannia* in two columns (one column on each side), at 25 knots – *quite a sight. Britannia* herself was steaming at a speed of 15 knots, so the resultant turbulence caused her to be buffeted about somewhat. All who were lucky enough to witness this impressive event commented in awe at the seamanship displayed - bearing in mind the ships passed with only about 1,000 ft between them.

The jackstay (the flag pole on the stern of the ship), was used to transfer Admiral Mountbatten by breeches buoy from his flagship *HMS Glasgow,* so that he could report the arrival of the fleet to Her Majesty. *This was quite dangerous and no doubt it is very rarely done these days due to Health and Safety Regulations.*

When *Britannia* and *Gothic* met in Grand Harbour, Valletta, Malta, The Queen's furniture and other effects were transferred from the *Gothic* onto *Britannia.* Some of these items included the light fittings and mirror in The Queen's Study on *Britannia* today.

Her Majesty made the decision not to have a permanent chaplain on board, so the Admiral stepped in for Sunday services to which all members of the crew could attend. On one occasion in his sermon, Vice Admiral Abel Smith (*Britannia's* first Admiral), referred to Her Majesty The Queen, Prince Philip, The Queen Mother, Prince Charles and all The Royal Family. Princess Anne is said to have turned to Her Majesty and expressed concern over his omission of her name, her comment caused a little hilarity amongst the congregation.

On 15th May, the *Britannia* sailed into the Pool of London to complete The Queen's Post Coronation Tour. A huge 'Welcome Home' sign was placed on Tower Bridge and the jibs of hundreds of cranes were raised as a sign of respect (in much the same way as they were in 2012 for the Diamond Jubilee). More than a million people lined the streets and the banks of the River Thames.

Also on this day, Vice Admiral Abel Smith received a Knighthood in the State Dining Room from Her Majesty, who used his sword to carry out the ceremony.

1955

On 28th June, following a successful State visit to Norway, *Britannia* was in Dundee, Scotland, where the two small Royal sailing yachts *Cowslip* (a Flying Fifteen racing yacht which is currently on display at *Britannia*), and *Bluebottle* (a Dragon Class racing yacht), were competing in the Tay Week Regatta. A few days later, *Britannia* docked in Granton, Edinburgh, for six days to coincide with the famous Edinburgh Festival.

It is often forgotten that The Queen is the Duchess of Edinburgh.

That year, following Cowes Week (the longest running and largest sailing regatta in the world), *Britannia* headed on the first of many Western Isles Cruises. This was one of the few times that The Royal Family could fully relax away from the press and public glare. They were able to unwind in complete peace and tranquillity. On those days barbecues, fishing, walks and painting were the order of the day.

Over the years the ship's crew kept detailed notes on the islands and beaches that they visited, so that they could be revisited or avoided in the future. Often the weather played an important role in the decision on where they would go the next day, particularly if there was a plan that relied on good weather - such as a barbecue.

In August, The Queen was walking in Upper Loch Torridon when she saw a young couple who did not recognise her. She also saw a shepherd who quite obviously did. As he approached her he doffed his cap, bowed his head slightly, addressing her as "Your Majesty" and remarked on what a perfect evening it was for a walk, before walking away apparently unaffected by her presence. The Queen thought that this was fantastic and enthusiastically recounted both tales on her return to *Britannia*.

1956

In March, the *Britannia* was involved in naval exercises just off Gibraltar, when she jammed the radio airwaves with the famous tune 'Britannia Rules the Waves'. This was effectively an early form of electronic countermeasures.

In July, she was sailing into Stockholm for a State visit, where an air display had been organised. She was running a little late due to dense fog and therefore had to maintain a considerably increased speed. The resultant bow wave caused some damage to pleasure craft moored on the river, costing around £100,000 to repair.

Fireworks displays often provided an important part of the entertainment onboard. For instance, on one occasion whilst off the Castle of Mey (The Queen Mother's residence on the North Coast of Scotland), a rocket misfired along the deck causing commotion amongst the crew and The Royal Party.

This year saw *Britannia* embark on the first of her world cruises, where she sailed almost 40,000 nautical miles in less than four months, visiting several remote communities.

When in the Southern Hemisphere Prince Philip chronicled his adventures in a book titled 'Birds from Britannia'. Whilst he was there he opened the Melbourne Olympic Games.

On 15th December, strong crosswinds caused *Britannia's* stern to collide with the wharf, when berthing in Lyttelton, New Zealand. This collision caused several metal plates and the lower gangway entrance doors to buckle. Luckily, no immediate repairs were required, and she was found to still be completely seaworthy.

Having experienced collisions similar to this myself, the forces involved are quite unbelievable – tearing into the metal plates of the ship just as easily as one would rip a piece of paper.

Prince Philip made a Christmas speech on the radio (prior to The Queen's Christmas broadcast from Sandringham), from The Queen's sitting room on board *Britannia*, about 9,000 miles from the United Kingdom - *quite a feat in those days.*

Two appendicitis operations were carried out on board in the South Atlantic Ocean. One involved the First Engineer from an Argentinian ship *SS Mabel Ryan,* and the other involved a scientist from the very remote Gough Island.
It was extremely fortunate for them that Britannia was around on these occasions.

1958

1958 saw the filming of the now famous Royal children's slide, which was located down the starboard side stairway to the Royal Deck. The shipwrights made the slide from wood and it was made slippery using salt water from a nearby fire hydrant and hose.

1959

In 1959, Her Majesty was on board *Britannia* to officially open the St Lawrence Seaway, which connects the Great Lakes to the Atlantic Ocean.

In preparation for the Canadian part of the tour, Canadian Naval personnel were boarded on *Britannia*. They included Petty Officer Auger (WRCNS), who was a clerk to the Press Secretary. She made history by being the first woman to don the official uniform of the Royal Yachtsman/Yachtswoman.

Also on board for the St Lawrence Seaway ceremonial opening were both, President Eisenhower from the United States and Prime Minister Diefenbaker from Canada.

During the planning of this, President Eisenhowers' security advisers were in contact with *Britannia*, and they requested accommodation for over fifty members of his Staff and Security Officers. They were informed in no uncertain terms, that they could only bring a maximum of three members of staff.

It was no doubt clearly explained that Her Majesty travelled with her own security and that would be sufficient.

In order to allow *Britannia* to sail through the St Lawrence Seaway, some modifications had to be made. The top 20 ft of the mainmast was modified so that it could be scandalised (lowered), as could the foremast aerial – thus reducing its height by about 3 ft. These two modifications allowed her to sail under the lower bridges, such as the Jacques Cartier Bridge. In addition to this, an Elm rubbing strip (120 ft x 9 in), was incorporated on both the port and starboard sides near to the waterline. This was to prevent the ships' sides from being scratched whilst negotiating the very narrow locks in the seaway. Following this trip, the rubbing strip remained as it was felt that the loss of the speed caused by it, was worth the gains it afforded by protecting the ship's side.

Whilst navigating the St Lawrence Seaway a notable incident occurred in one of the tight locks. This was when a large rubber fender was squeezed very tightly (as *Britannia* was only just able to get into the lock due to her width), and burst. The resultant noise sounded like gunfire. This caused the American Close Protection Officers to panic and reach for their side arms. All became calm when everyone realised what had happened.

The Yacht also suffered from an intrusion of bats in the Royal Apartments and ventilation ducts. Once Her Majesty had retired for the night, the crew set about releasing the offending creatures by the quietest means possible so as not to disturb Her Majesty.

On the Seaway there were no rules regarding the disposal of waste, so it was merely discharged overboard. On subsequent trips there, the rules had changed which meant that waste could no longer be disposed of using *Britannia's* previous methods. However, *Britannia* had limited means of storing waste water so portable toilets were taken on board - *of course, these were not for Royal use!*

From the Seaway, she continued south on to the Welland Canal, west past Detroit and all the way to Chicago on Lake Michigan (there is a photograph in the Whispering Corridor adjacent to the Admiral's Quarters, of the *Britannia* sailing under the Mackinac Bridge, which connects the two parts of the US State of Michigan). Later she sailed on to Port Arthur (now known as Thunder Bay), at the western end of Lake Superior, where The Queen disembarked to complete her Canadian Tour - *that is just about as far west as you can get in Canada by water.*

1961

On 29th April, *Britannia* sailed into Cagliari on the island of Sardinia, when unfortunately, a four-inch wire cable became entangled in the port side propeller. So, divers complete with special cutting gear, and the assistance of the crew from *HMS Surprise*, managed to free the offending wire. The following day, the Italian press had a bit of a field day with banner headlines such as 'Britannia Spaghetti'.

1963

Britannia was in the Pacific heading for Tahiti when she answered an emergency call from *SS Glenmore*. The ship's boiler had suffered a flashback resulting in a few injuries. Once again, the Sick Bay was put into action to deal with a crew member who had suffered severe burns.

Later that year The Queen Mother visited Castletown on the Isle of Man, where she was gifted a Manx cat, which in due course found a good home with the family of one of *Britannia's* engineers. This was just one of the many special gifts the Royals were graciously given throughout their travels.

1965

The 1965 refit included air conditioning units being fitted in the crews' quarters, which ultimately made this area much more comfortable for them. Along with other modifications the cost of the entire refit came to just over £300,000.

1967

Whilst crossing the Atlantic, heading for Canada, some racing pigeons landed on the Bridge. As they were used to being handled by humans, they were all housed in the flag lockers, which just happened to be the perfect size. One of the birds laid an egg which was successfully incubated in the Engine Room.

On a very sombre note, in July, the extremely ill Captain of the bulk carrier *SS Container Forwarder*, came on board for treatment. Unfortunately, despite great efforts from *Britannia's* medical staff, they were unsuccessful, and he passed away. The National flag of America was draped over him and one of the crew's musicians piped him onto one of the motor cutters, and he was transferred ashore.

1968

This year, the Labour Government oversaw tough spending cuts. The Admiralty's budget and consequently *Britannia*, all felt the effects of this. An offer was made privately by The Queen and Prince Philip to the Government to relinquish the Yacht, in an effort to reduce public expenditure, and to show that even The Royal Family were being impacted by the economic struggle. However, this offer was refused by the Prime Minister, Harold Wilson. Efforts were made to ensure that whilst *Britannia* was not on Royal duty, she was put to good use. For example, she was involved in many naval exercises and Sea Days - this was when businessmen from the countries that *Britannia* was visiting were invited on board for discussions and meetings with their British counterparts.

1970

On 31st July, the last rum issue was given to the Royal Navy, and because of this, the day is now known by Royal Navy Seamen as 'Black Tot Day'. This was inevitably a sad day for the crew. However, it was replaced by cans of beer, although unfortunately for the crew they had to be bought!

1971

In February, when *Britannia* was heading towards Easter Island in the Pacific, Prince Philip requested that Engineer Commander Trowbridge (later promoted to Admiral), join him on the Verandah Deck. The Prince asked the Commander if he could see any differences in the two sides of the wake. On further inspection the Commander noted that each side of the wake appeared slightly different. *Britannia* was brought to a stop to enable divers to go down and examine the ships' stabilisers. It was confirmed that part of one of the stabilisers had worked loose and a temporary repair was carried out. *A very good observation by the Prince.*

In March, whilst going alongside at Victoria, Canada, one of *Britannia's* crew members threw a light mooring line which struck a lady spectator. Thankfully she was not injured, but along with her husband she was later invited on board the *Britannia* by way of an apology. *As I am sure you can imagine, they were both delighted.*

1972

During the 1972 refit, the main focus was to replace and upgrade the crew's accommodation. Improvements were made to several essential areas, including the ship's dining hall and the crews' bathrooms. In addition to this, the Yotties were given beds in the form of triple bunks instead of hammocks - *quite a luxury in comparison.*

On 24th March, *Britannia* was in Port Louis, Mauritius, where two Soviet survey vessels were dressed (with flags flying fore and aft), as a sign of respect to The Queen and Prince Philip.
When a Naval ship is dressed, there is a specific order for the flags to be in, which is laid down by the Admiralty. No doubt this stopped crew members from sending each other messages.

1973

In December, whilst in the South Pacific Ocean, *Britannia* engaged in an immense 1,200-mile tow of the stricken tanker *Blue Rover.* The tanker had suffered an unfortunate fire caused by fractured fuel pipes. Initially, *Britannia* didn't have a sufficient amount of fuel to engage in the tow, so the crew created a means of pumping the tanker's fuel across to *Britannia* using an old diesel pump from the tanker. This ultimately enabled *Britannia* to tow the *Blue Rover* all the way to Tahiti.

1975

On 8th January, (three days early due to other commitments), *Britannia* celebrated the 21st Anniversary of her being commissioned. Silver coins were struck for all the original members of the crew and one was presented to Her Majesty.

In February, *Britannia* sailed into Cozumel, Mexico. The seas were very rough, and it was uncertain whether or not The Queen would be able to get ashore. The Royal Party were eventually conveyed ashore in the Barge from *Britannia's* anchorage. There were two incidents caused by the extreme weather, these being: one of the seamen suffered a broken wrist, whilst another fell overboard from one of the assisting vessels.

On a happier note, when Her Majesty continued on to Mexico City, the streets were crowded with nearly one and a half million well-wishers.

In May, as the Royal Yacht was sailing into Portsmouth, The Queen Mother disembarked onto the Royal Barge where she was to be taken ashore. As she was stepping off the Barge there was a sudden jolting of the vessel. This caused her to lose her balance so significantly that she let go of her handbag, which tumbled into the water. The Barge Officer managed to recover the now rather wet bag, and a few days later he received a letter thanking him personally. This hand-written letter is said to have been accompanied by a small silver gift from The Queen Mother herself.

1976

On 6th July, *Britannia* sailed up the Delaware River into Philadelphia. Later she sailed for New York, berthing at the famous Pier 88 and then onto Boston, where she was met by a twenty-one-gun salute from the *USS Constitution* (affectionally known by the Americans as *Old Ironsides*). Later, she headed for Halifax for the start of The Queen's Tour of Canada and then on to Montreal for Her Majesty to open the Olympic Games.

1977

This was a busy year for *Britannia* as it saw The Queen's Silver Jubilee and she completed her 6th circumnavigation of the world.

In October, whilst in the Atlantic Ocean, Concorde carried out a low-level flypast. A photograph was taken of The Queen and Prince Philip on the Verandah Deck with Concorde in the background. British Airways used one of these photographs for advertising purposes.

1978

By late 1978, the Rolls Royce (see page 42), was no longer required to be taken on Royal Tours, however the garage did not lie empty. Not only was it used as a beer store, it also housed lobster pots and creels during the Western Isles Cruises. The local fisherman told the crew where the best places were to catch lobster, so fresh lobster was often the order of the day.

1981

In 1981, Prince Charles married Lady Diana Spencer. They boarded *Britannia* in Gibraltar for a two-week Mediterranean cruise, which took in the Greek Islands and ended with a visit to President Sadat in Port Said, Egypt.

1982

In 1982, Her Majesty gave her permission for *Britannia* to be used in the Falklands conflict. However, there are three main reasons why *Britannia* did not go:

- The first, was that she would have been an easy and high value target.
- The second, was that all the other ships in the task force (with the exception of the aircraft carrier and task force flagship - *HMS Hermes*), were powered by fuel oil. (It was not until 1986 that *Britannia* was eventually converted from fuel furnace oil to fuel oil).
- The third was that she was not hermetically sealed (airtight) against NBC threats (Nuclear, Biological and Chemical Warfare).

These issues meant that the *SS Uganda* was converted to a hospital ship instead.

The 28^h March saw the 40th anniversary commemorations of the raid on St Nazaire in France. (In 1942 St Nazaire had been occupied by German forces when the Allies planned to destroy the main dry dock. The mission to destroy the dock was successful, however during the raid the Allied forces suffered heavy casualties). For the anniversary The Duke of Edinburgh (who is a patron of the St Nazaire Society), arranged that half of the survivors were transported on *Britannia* to the commemorations in St Nazaire, whilst the other half made the return journey.

In November, whilst in Western Samoa, *Britannia's* crew showed their expertise and firefighting skills when they helped extinguish a fire in a large warehouse, near to where she was berthed. The main concern was that the fire might spread to a nearby oil tank - which could have had catastrophic consequences. Luckily, this was not the case and the fire was successfully put out in around an hour.

1983

In 1983, *Britannia* went to Long Beach, California. Bad weather caused heavy flooding on many of the local roads, which meant that an ordinary limousine was unsuitable for Her Majesty to use. As a replacement, a large shabby bus (which was capable of navigating the floods), was requisitioned and Her Majesty was given a pair of wellies and asked to ride on the bus - *I am sure Her Majesty would have greatly enjoyed this.*

1986

In January, *Britannia* was ordered to Aden, where she evacuated over a thousand foreign nationals from civil war torn South Yemen, across the Gulf of Aden to Djibouti. This was known as 'Operation Balsac'. As part of this, the Royal Apartments had to be stripped out and the Royal Bridge became the Operations Room. On arrival, there was heavy conflict. A Soviet vessel challenged *Britannia's* right to enter the waters, but the challenge was ignored by the Admiral and *Britannia* sailed in flags flying and floodlit. Her jolly boats (tenders), were used to transport the evacuees from the shore to the fast motor launches. They in turn conveyed them to *Britannia* where they were given essential supplies. French and Soviet Liaison Officers were taken on board so that all countries involved could communicate with one another.

I was recently told by a retired Ministry of Defence employee that the Russian Ambassador was also rescued, and he demanded that the Admiral contact the Kremlin immediately – this was able to be done within 30 seconds!

Messages of congratulations on a job well done were sent to the crew from The Queen and Prime Minister (copies of these messages are on display in the Petty Officers' Mess on board *Britannia* today). The Queen gave the order "Splice the mainbrace", which meant all the crew were able to have an extra drink in the form of a triple tot of rum. *Britannia* then resumed her course to Australia and New Zealand.

Later, whilst sailing for Cairns, *Britannia* was involved in the rescue of a nearby yacht, the *African Queen*. This involved her responding to an urgent call from the two crew members onboard, who explained that their yacht was taking on excessive amounts of water and her engines had stopped working. An urgent rescue was essential, so *Britannia* quickly responded and once again the Sick Bay was put to good use, when one of the crew members of the yacht collapsed. He was later transferred to hospital by helicopter for further treatment.

On 9th March, *Britannia* was sailing off New Zealand when Halley's Comet passed. A spectacular sight, although unfortunately, the view of the comet was only partially visible due to intermittent clouds.

In October, The Queen made an historic visit to Shanghai, China. During the visit, a State Banquet was held in honour of President Li Xiannian.

1987

1987 saw *Britannia's* biggest refit completed at a cost of over £20 million. Taking ten months to complete, there was an incredible amount of work carried out throughout the Yacht. It included the extraction of around 7,000 square yards of asbestos, 25 tonnes of paint was scraped off and around 20 miles of new wiring was installed. As well as this, 14 miles of Burmese teak deck was removed and replaced with brand new Burmese teak decking, which was specially sourced. In addition to this, the Royal Apartments were entirely renovated giving *Britannia* a new lease of life.

1988

In April, The Queen made a special visit to Brisbane to commemorate the 200th anniversary of settlers in Australia. Whilst alongside a jetty *Britannia* was subject to some unsightly vandalism - under the cover of darkness, the phrase 'end the killing times', was smeared in paint on her port bow. The paint was very quickly removed, however this was not done before the press had captured their headlines.

1989

There was a visit to *Britannia* from the House of Lords and the House of Commons Defence Study Group. Questions were starting to be asked in Parliament about *Britannia's* future, specifically whether or not she would be undergoing another expensive refit in 1997.

When in Cowes, the yacht *Scorcher* came a little too close to the white ensign at the stern of *Britannia*, whereby her mast became entangled in the flag, causing it to be ripped off.

On 22nd September, an IRA terrorist bomb blast killed 11 and injured 22 Royal Marine Bandsmen at Deal Barracks in Kent. *Britannia's* crew raised nearly £2,000 for the victims' families by holding one of her well-known concerts.

1990

In March, a routine inspection of the boilers revealed small holes and cracks in one of the boiler's internal tubes. This was one of many signs of *Britannia* now showing her age.

1991

In April, *Britannia* navigated some distance up into the Amazon. The river is quite wide in parts, with shallow and muddy waters, making it extremely difficult to predict the correct channel, and to generally navigate without specialist knowledge. Therefore, in order to sail safely, an Amazonian Indian pilot was contracted to help navigate the river.

In May, when *Britannia* docked in Miami, soapy bubbles (or something similar), were observed being emitted from the Yacht by the local pollution authorities. They were quick to react and slapped a $10,000 fine on her, and ordered the Admiral to sail out of the harbour within a two-hour period. The Admiral had to request the involvement of the White House to allow the Yacht to remain for the evening State Dinner which she was hosting (The main guests included four past Presidents: Ford, Carter, Reagan, Bush and the current President at the time - Bill Clinton).

Her Majesty does not deal with money as it is organised by her staff, so when she was told of the fine she showed great concern to the Admiral and questioned how the ship would be able to pay. The Admiral with a completely straight face, told her that he had put much thought into the matter, and he suggested that they should start saving up the empty plastic bottles of ginger beer and tonic water. Then, once Her Majesty had her next bath they should fill the bottles with her bath water and sell them to the Americans for $1,000 each. Luckily, Her Majesty was very amused by this suggestion.

I told this story to an American visitor who found it most amusing and said that he would have paid $10,000 for just one bottle!

Whilst anchored off Loggerhead Key, Florida, an unwelcome phone call was received from the East Midlands Police. They were informed that a call had been received, stating that a bomb had been placed on *Britannia* about a metre below the waterline, which was timed to go off imminently. Her Majesty showed great concern during the phone call and had asked the Admiral if there was a problem. He explained quite calmly that if a bomb were to go off, they would just have to spend a few months grounded whilst any damage was fixed, as they were only in about a metre of water below the keel - *I am sure Her Majesty found this explanation most reassuring!* Checks by the crews' divers revealed that the ship was in fact clear, so the call had been a hoax.

Whilst en route to Bermuda, *Britannia* launched a boat to pick up a refugee who had escaped from the Communist Cuban regime, with the intention of paddling to the USA to claim asylum. The 21-year-old male was lucky to be alive, as he had been floating on a 3ft x 2ft x 2ft, makeshift polystyrene raft and had run out of essential supplies.

In June, there was an unscheduled additional Royal engagement. However, as budgets had already been set there was no money available from the Admiralty and hence no fuel could be bought to cover this. An enterprising call to the Chief Executive of Amoco (an oil company), proved fruitful and the fuel was supplied. This allowed the engagement to be kept.

This was the year of now famous scene, when Princess Diana and Prince Charles boarded *Britannia* in Toronto and happily greeted Prince William and Prince Harry (see page 41).

1992

In June, a message was received from the Commander in Chief Fleet, stating that the Yacht's budget was to be cut by 10% and her crew numbers were to be cut by 5% in December.

The Conservative Government of the time set plans in motion for a new Royal Yacht that would be around two thirds of the size, with a much smaller crew of around 125. She would be capable of covering 4 to 5 thousand miles (where *Britannia* was generally only capable of 2,000 to 2,500 miles − not even enough to cross the Atlantic without refuelling). Additionally, there would be state-of-the-art conference facilities, along with a helicopter landing pad. It was to have an estimated cost in the region of £80 million - which would reduce if companies supplying equipment could use it as advertising. A subsequent General Election in 1997 saw the Labour Government, under Prime Minister Tony Blair, come to power and consequently the idea of a new Royal Yacht was shelved.

In June, *Britannia* sailed up the Garonne River into Bordeaux for a State visit with President Mitterrand. During the visit, 300 visitors came on board for a reception and to watch the Marine band performing 'Beat the Retreat' on the quayside. ('Beat the Retreat' is a superb display of military music, precision drill and colour, which dates back to the 16th century and is regarded as a piece of living history). In order to counterbalance the weight of the visitors, one of the Yachts' boats was put out on its davits (which was usual practice specifically for these types of events). Unfortunately, as soon as the band stopped playing, a fireworks display - which had been organised by the President - began on the opposite side of the river. As a result, all the visitors wandered over to the other side of *Britannia* causing her to roll alarmingly!

1993

On 26th May, to commemorate the 50th Anniversary of the Battle of the Atlantic, another fleet review was carried out off Liverpool. This time the Elder Brethren of Trinity House was forced to relinquish its right of place ahead of the Royal Yacht due to a force 8 gale -*the weather in the United Kingdom stops for nobody, not even Royalty!* Following this, *Britannia* docked outside the iconic Royal Liver Building on the River Mersey, Liverpool.

By way of explanation, Trinity House were incorporated in 1514 by King Henry VIII. They were initially concerned with pilotage in the Thames, which until that point, appears to have been very haphazard and ungoverned. Nowadays they are responsible for, amongst other things, the maintenance of lighthouses and buoys in England and Wales (the Northern Lighthouse Board have a similar responsibility for Scotland and The Isle of Man).

The Trinity House Vessel, Patricia, was built in Leith at Henry Robbs shipbuilders. Henry Robbs was actually on the site of Ocean Terminal where *Britannia* is now permanently moored.

1994

On 10th February, *Britannia* sailed into the Hudson River, New York. The river was covered by a layer of ice, which scraped her paintwork and blocked some filters. As a result, her emergency power generator 'Chitty Chitty Bang Bang', was called into action. This generator had been taken from the submarine HMS *Vampire*, which was scrapped in 1950.

On 22nd June, the Defence Secretary Malcolm Rifkind announced that there would be no major refit for *Britannia*, and that she would be "paid off" (decommissioned), in 1997. One reason given was that the refit would cost in the region of £18 million, and that no guarantees could be given that her serviceability would be defect-free following this.

October saw *Britannia* in St Petersburg for The Queen's State visit to Russia, where she met President Yeltsin and his wife Naina. A State Banquet was held in their honour.

It was clear to the crew that the Russian Navy was in a poor way and morale was very low. Many of the ships they saw laid up were being used by sailors and their families as they had nowhere else to live and had not been paid for several months.

1995

In February, *Britannia* embarked on a State visit to South Africa. This was to be her 85th Official State visit and her final one. Nelson Mandela came on board on 21st March whilst in Durban– *quite a spectacular, historical and memorable occasion.*

On *Britannia's* return, Rear Admiral Woodard (*Britannia's* ninth and last Admiral), was knighted in Her Majesty's sitting room.

1996

On 6th May, whilst crossing the Bay of Biscay, two abnormally large waves crashed across the forecastle (pronounced fo'c'sle), of *Britannia*. This stripped a 16ft section from the starboard bulwark. As a result, she was forced to go to Portsmouth for the repairs to be carried out. *I'm told that she went alongside port side, to avoid any embarrassment.*

1997

On 28th February, in the Gulf of Oman, *Britannia* collided with the Royal Fleet Auxiliary Ship the *Bayleaf,* whilst receiving supplies at sea in calm waters. No doubt the pull-push forces between both vessels, (due to their proximity), were at least partially to blame. In fact, some damage was caused all along the starboard side of *Britannia,* both above and below the waterline. She underwent immediate repairs in Karachi,

Pakistan, and then spent two weeks in Singapore undergoing more substantial repairs.

The 23rd June saw *Britannia's* last official duty when Prince Charles, accompanied by Governor Chris Patten, handed Hong Kong back to China. She sailed out in the late evening and thereafter headed to Manilla in the Philippines, where Prince Charles and Governor Patten disembarked. *Britannia* continued on home via Gibraltar.

On 28th July, an enormous fireworks display was organised to signify her departure from Gibraltar for the very last time.

On this deployment, the Yacht had completed an extraordinary journey. She had undertaken a noteworthy 28 visits to as many as 17 different countries and had hosted numerous events. She made her last journey into Portsmouth signalling the end of her working life

Later that year, 19 members of The Royal Family (at different times), embarked onto *Britannia* for their last farewell to her, as she did a final UK wide tour. The Yacht called in at the ports of Devonport, Cardiff, Belfast, Liverpool, Glasgow, Aberdeen, Newcastle and London.

END OF AN ERA FOLLOWED BY A NEW LIFE

The 21ˢᵗ November 1997 marked *Britannia's* final day in harbour in London, before decommissioning. As per Naval tradition she flew her Paying Off Pennant, which was the same length as her overall length (412 ft 3 in). Traditionally it would have been one and a half times her length plus a foot for every year of service, but one times her length was deemed appropriate on this occasion.

At 1055 hours on 22ⁿᵈ November 1997, *Britannia* entered Portsmouth harbour, at which time there was a fly past of helicopters and sea harriers. At 1135 hours, her engines were ordered to stop for the last time.

At 1501 hours on 11ᵗʰ December 1997, Her Majesty The Queen was ceremonially piped off *Britannia* for the final time and *Britannia* was effectively decommissioned from that point. The events unfolded in the form of a Sunday service, along with a final 'Beat the Retreat', the 'Sunset', and a heart rending edition of 'Auld Lang Syne'. This historic spectacle was televised and watched by millions. At 1537 hours *Britannia's* flags were lowered. The Royal Standard was later lowered when Her Majesty had left the area.

In The Queen and Prince Phillip's farewell letter to the crew they said,

'...It is with sadness that we must now say goodbye to Britannia...'

I think it is fair to say that The Queen shed a tear on that day, as did the whole Commonwealth and no doubt many millions across the world who had their own personal memories of Britannia.

The next question was what to do with the Royal Yacht. The Admiralty thought that it would be more dignified for her to be scrapped, whilst others thought that she should be scuttled. However, it was decided that she would be saved for the Nation as a Visitor Attraction. There were seven bids for her and Leith came out on top, as it was described as the most imaginative bid (not to mention that it was to be a self-supporting bid). The other bids were from Portsmouth (her home port), Glasgow (where she was built), London (three individual bids), and Manchester. In addition to being effectively a museum, the plan put forward by Leith Port Authority was to include evening events, along with both morning and evening private tours. Leith was undergoing major regeneration at the time, which included redevelopment of the dock area and the building of the large shopping centre, Ocean Terminal, where *Britannia* is now permanently berthed.

On 1st May 1998 she was sold to Leith Port Authority, lock, stock and barrel, for her mere scrap value of £250,000. Her decommissioning in Portsmouth involved many things including: decommissioning her engines, removing equipment, cleaning her fuel tanks and filling them with water for additional ballast. She was towed to Leith by a tug, on a journey which saw force 8 gales and took five days to complete with a 600m towing line.

Finally, on 5th May she arrived at Leith, her new and current home. She underwent a £2.5 million alteration into a Visitor Attraction which is accessible to all. The *Britannia* Charitable Trust was formed, and the first Visitor Centre was opened on 19th October 1998. In her first month she saw over 30,000 visitors, ending her first year with over 436,000. Early 2002, saw her reach her one millionth visitor and in the summer of 2016, she welcomed her fifth millionth.

Today, not only can you do a tour of the Yacht yourself, taking in the region of 1 ½ - 2 hours *(although it took me close to 5 hours, when I first visited her out of pure interest and enjoyment).*
There are around 90 private events each year from anywhere between 2 and 520 guests. On these occasions, guests receive the red-carpet

treatment. They are often piped on board via the Royal Brow, from where they then enter the State Anteroom and are perhaps offered a glass of Champagne and a canape or two by one of her immaculately dressed Butlers. All before making themselves at home in the State Drawing Room, where the Welmar mini-grand piano provides some ambience. They are then taken on a brief tour of the ships' highlights, which may include the Wardroom, Admirals' Quarters, The Rolls Royce and finally The Queen's Private Apartments. Thereafter, there is a fantastic meal to be had with synchronised service from the excellent staff and perhaps some background music played on a harp. To complete the evening, there may be a band playing on the Royal Deck with dancing and fireworks.

GENERAL INFORMATION

During the construction of the Royal Yacht numerous requirements were made by the Admiralty. Perhaps one of the most demanding of these was a requirement for economy. Another requirement was that the Yacht had to be capable of being quickly converted into a hospital ship in time of war. It also required stabilisers, as well as air conditioning for the wards (this was the area of the Royal Apartments). In addition to this there had to be a considerable sized laundry, along with a need for relatively high speed and a minimum range of 2,000 miles.

Her design specification included a clipper bow and cruiser stern with a semi bulbous bow (which proved to give increased performance at speeds over 18 knots).

Construction included transverse frames with 2 ft spaces, along with the construction of web frames and beam networks in the State Rooms, removing any requirement for unattractive columns.

Britannia is one of the final fully riveted ships in existence, having been one of the last ships to be built with this technique. The rivets are barely visible on the hull as they were countersunk, chamfered, filler was applied and then covered with six coats of paint.

All the decks have a 9-inch camber which increased her strength and would aid water flow if the Yacht was flooded.

The *Britannia's* Royal Deck (where the Tea Room is now located), was specially strengthened to allow helicopters to land. This would require the removal of the mizzen mast, however it was never used for such a purpose.

Britannia is fitted with two Gyro stabilised electro-hydraulic stabilisers, which were designed and built in Granton, Edinburgh, by Denny Brown. They reduced the roll from 20 degrees to 6 degrees. There is a model of them in the Engine Room of *Britannia* today.

I am often asked if Britannia has a golden rivet. I can confirm that she does. It is located in the Engine Room under the viewing platform behind some recently fitted equipment, making it quite difficult to see.

Initially, two 3lb Saluting Guns were carried on the Bridge deck, as it had been traditional practice to fire a gun twice a day when The Queen was onboard, with the Standard Flying. However, the guns were removed soon after she was commissioned.

The working part of the ship and crew's accommodation is located to the front of the mainmast, whilst the Royal Apartments and Household Staff Quarters are located to the rear.

For a very short period of time, *Britannia* had a ship's cat called Fluff, which found its way on board at John Brown's shipyard. During *Britannia's* first voyage she faced severe weather conditions, resulting in Fluff being extremely sick. Due to this, Fluff was quickly discharged from the ship and set ashore.

On many occasions *Britannia* was subjected to severe weather. The worst conditions included 20 ft tall waves and a swell which was 400 ft long (almost the length of the Yacht). *Imagine the centre of the Yacht perched on top of a crest with her bow and stern out of the water, and then her bow crashing straight into the next crest -quite uncomfortable.*

As the forecastle bulwarks were only 4 ft high, she shipped some very heavy seas. Early in her commission, these bulwarks were heightened to 6 ft, which saw a great improvement in the ship's stability.

On 15th January 1954, *Britannia* was subjected to particularly bad storms, so much so that the anchors dragged. Due to this, she was forced to go underway off the Isle of Arran on the West Coast of Scotland.

There were two other notable anchor incidents worth mentioning:

- The first occurred in 1959 whilst near Montreal. The anchor chain fractured causing the anchor and about four shackles of chain to be lost. The failure of the chain was put down to either; metal fatigue or a manufacturing defect. Attempts to recover it proved fruitless.
- The second incident took place in 1963 whilst The Queen and Prince Philip were onboard. *Britannia* was in York Harbour, Newfoundland, when an anchor fluke snapped off in extreme weather. The noise was heard, and the ship shuddered, but the damage was not in evidence until the anchor was weighed (pulled up). The shipwrights on board made a wooden fluke - which once painted and fixed to the remains of the anchor - disguised the problem. From a distance it was able to fool everyone.

There were four Royal honeymoons on board: Princess Margaret to Antony Armstrong-Jones, Princess Anne to Captain Mark Phillips, Prince Charles to Lady Diana Spencer and Prince Andrew to Sarah Ferguson. As a result of the numerous honeymoons in *Britannia's* service, the Yotties often nicknamed *Britannia* 'The Love Boat'. However regrettably, all of these marriages ended in divorce.

Unfortunately for the Royal Marines, in the early days there was no specific accommodation for them, so they had to use the crew's mess to sling their hammocks.

A Royal Air Force Queens's flight exchange to *Britannia* saw 23 RAF personnel onboard. Exchanges such as these went on throughout *Britannia's* service. For instance, when *Britannia* was due to go on a foreign tour, personnel from that country were often taken on board for a few weeks and were used for liaison purposes and to provide very valuable local knowledge.

Silent orders and hand signals such as semaphore were used on board, as they were generally very efficient and showed the utmost decorum. Unfortunately, on one occasion they led to miscommunication whereby three boats were mistakenly lowered into heavy seas, when the order had meant to say not to release the boats.

Britannia was indeed expensive to run – the annual bill for the year 1987/1988 (which included a 10 month long major refit), was over £22 million. Yearly costs varied depending on *Britannia's* commitments for that particular year and if she was undergoing any kind of refit. These costs should probably be weighed against the income she generated in the form of advertising the United Kingdom across the world. Not to mention the numerous business deals that were made and sometimes signed onboard.

During the 1987 refit, all 14 miles of Burmese teak decking was replaced. It is 2 inches thick and bolted to the steel decks beneath. It took three months to pick the correct replacement timber as it was required to have the correct shade and grain. Prior to the refit some of the decking was down to an inch thick due to the constant scrubbing of the deck by the crew, by what was known as Holystoning. This was where a crewman would get down on his hands and knees (as if praying - hence Holy), and scrub the deck with a piece of sandstone (hence stoning), and copious amounts of salt water. The decks were sealed with caulking (the process of forcing hemp rope soaked in tar into the gaps between planks, with a hammer and chisel). Awkward joins at the edges of the ship (devil), where a crew member was perhaps suspended over the side to do the caulking, gave vent to the term 'between the devil and the deep blue sea'.

I am told that one enterprising crew member managed to obtain some scraps of the old decking from which he made a chair, that now sits proudly in his living room. A friend of his offered him £1,500 for it but this was politely refused.

In *Britannia's* final years, costs were reduced by replacing the Admiral with a Commodore – giving a salary saving of approximately £7,000 per year. *Although I am told the resultant cost to change letterheads and other formal matters to include the Commodores' details, far outweighed any savings that were made.*

The Royal Barge is 40 ft long (12.5m), and is powered by twin 125hp Foden diesel engines, allowing her to reach a top speed of 20 knots. She was effectively decommissioned in 1997 at the same time as *Britannia,* although she was recommissioned for The Queen's Diamond Jubilee in 2012.

On one occasion the sewage tank alarms went off. The way to overcome this problem was for a crew member to merely crack a particular valve about a quarter of a turn. Unfortunately, the crew member sent to do the job misunderstood what he had to do, and he fully opened the valve. This caused the whole of the lower deck to be flooded with raw sewage to a depth of 2 ft in places. On hearing of the problem, the Admiral attended with very helpful advice which consisted of instructing the men to "clear that up!".

Officers were usually drafted to *Britannia* on a two-year secondment whilst the Admirals served for approximately five years.

Seamen who volunteered to be members of *Britannia's* crew were put through a rigorous procedure, including interviews and vetting. They joined for an initial six months, which was then extended by a further six months and then an additional probationary year. Thereafter, on satisfactory completion of the two years, they became permanent members of the Royal Yacht Service. They were then able to serve on board for as long as they were required.

The longest serving crew member on board *Britannia* was Coxswain Ellis Norrell MVO RVM or "Norrie" as he was known by Her Majesty. He served for 34 years, from 1954 until 1988. He started his service on board as an Able Seaman and progressed all the way up through the ranks to Coxswain of the Royal Barge. He often took Prince Charles and Princess Anne under his wing, and on one occasion taught them how to fish for mackerel.

The second longest serving member was Albert "Dixie" Deane MBE RVM with 26 years service. He is one of the founders of the Association of Royal Yachtsmen.

Britannia is the Headquarters of the Association of Royal Yachtsmen. In May of each year, around 50 Yachtsmen return to *Britannia* for 'Yotties Week', in which they undertake a range of maintenance work on board alongside the current maintenance crew. They also hold an annual dinner on board towards the end of the year. There were just short of 3,300 Officers and Crew throughout *Britannia's* service.

It was a requirement that all crew members should behave correctly whilst ashore and onboard. Offences such as being absent without leave and being drunk on duty would lead to immediate expulsion from the Yacht and a single ticket home. However misdemeanours of a minor nature were often dealt with on board.

On one occasion, one of *Britannia's* Stokers was instructed to dispose of a box filled with oily rags. He immediately did so by throwing them over the starboard side of the ship – with no thought or care towards the environment (which was not uncommon in those days). At this point the Yacht was doing in the region of 20 knots, so the rags were blown straight back onboard. Much to the Stoker's horror, one of the rags landed on the decking directly in front of the Royal Apartment's entrance, causing a 2-inch square stain on the teak decking. Immediately he panicked thinking that his career on the *Britannia* could be over. In an attempt to fix the issue, he spent the next five hours scrubbing and sanding down the affected area. The following day, he found himself in front of his Commanding Officer being disciplined for his mistake. He was initially reprimanded, but then to his surprise the Commanding Officer said, "I'm not sure if I should continue to chastise you for the next twenty minutes or perhaps congratulate you in showing me just how bad the rest of the deck is!". Fortunately for the Stoker he did not lose his job, and he continued to serve on board for many more years.

Still to this day, if you look very closely, you can just see the area where the rag landed as it is light in colour and slightly indented.

Stokers and seamen were often detailed to look after and entertain the Royal children. They would teach them how to helm the Yacht, aswell as other seamanship and survival-at-sea-skills. In addition to this they would perhaps teach them how to tie knots. They would also organise games or treasure hunts for them. From time to time the children were also involved in doing a little maintenance.

In 1954, whilst in the Irish Sea en-route to the Isle of Man, a football game between Prince Charles and a crew member took place on the Verandah Deck. One of Prince Charles' shots was a little off target and the ball was kicked overboard. A message was quickly relayed to the Bridge and *Britannia* was stopped. A full operation was launched to retrieve the ball, which was duly handed back to Charles, who immediately kicked it back overboard - *of course he did!* Needless to say, he was told that *Britannia* would not be stopped again.

Britannia's resident photographer (known as Snaps), was always a senior member of the ship's crew who had his own 8 ft by 5 ft dark room onboard. Snaps had quite a job especially when photographs of The Duke of Edinburgh were required, because as soon as The Duke sat down he wanted the photograph to be taken immediately. Some examples of Snaps' photographs can be seen in *Britannia's* Visitor Centre and in various places onboard.

Throughout *Britannia* there are photographs of foreign Naval ships from all corners of the world. For example, the Canadian ship *HMCN Haida* (now a Museum ship in Ontario), which is located in the Sergeant's Mess, and the Australian Navy's *HMAN Torrens*, which is pictured near to The Duke's bedroom (she was used as a target in 1999 and was sunk by a torpedo during live firing trials).

Another photograph of interest shows the tug *Airedale* off Gibraltar. In the foreground, Prince Charles and Princess Diana can be seen on *Britannia*, heading off into the Mediterranean on their honeymoon. This is located in the Warrant Officer's Mess.

When in Portsmouth (her home port), *Britannia* would moor alongside at H mooring on Whale Island. The crew would generally work Monday to Friday and start their duty at 0700, with an early afternoon finish. Many of the crew lived locally which meant they could return home after their shift.

Prior to entering port, *Britannia* would often head for heavy rain showers to wash off any salt accumulations, so that she would arrive looking her best. *Although it is also said that she was often washed from the funnel down with fresh water prior to entering port.*

Lifeboats were launched by use of gravity davits (which in the case of an emergency required no power - they were merely unlocked and lowered by use of a brake). Once the lifeboat touches the water an offload mechanism automatically releases the boat (which can also be released manually if required). There are two means of recovering the lifeboats. The first is both exhausting and time consuming as it involves manually winching them up with a large winding handle. The second involves the use of a portable electric motor which attaches to the winching mechanism.
When I served in the Merchant Navy I had to wind the lifeboats up many times, so I know first-hand how difficult and tiring this task is!

In 1962, Her Majesty and Prince Philip purchased *Bloodhound* – the famous ocean-going racing yacht. She was manufactured in 1936 by Camper and Nicholsons and is 63 ft long, with a 65 ft mast and weighs 34 tons. Her racing pedigree from her early years is nothing short of superb, with numerous wins including the Fastnet Race. The yacht remained in The Royal Family's ownership until 1969, and was often raced at Cowes and taken on their yearly Western Isles Cruise. Prince Charles and Princess Anne learned how to sail on her, and children from various societies and clubs had their first taste of sailing onboard. *Bloodhound* is now owned by Britannia Charitable Trust and is usually moored alongside *Britannia*.

In May 1998, following her decommissioning in Portsmouth, *Britannia* was towed to Leith - her new home. On her arrival, she went to dry-dock where she was painted and cathodic protection (40 cathodes) was installed below the waterline. Her two spare propellers were placed in a shed on the quayside for safekeeping. Unfortunately, both propellers were stolen and only one was ever recovered. The blades from the recovered propeller had been cut off and cut into small manageable pieces so that it would have easier for the thieves to take them to the scrap metal merchant. The propellers were made of Manganese Bronze, worth about £5,000 per tonne - at today's prices. It was not possible to repair the propeller so instead, two 'Norrie' statues were cast from the pieces, which can now be seen on the quayside beside *Britannia*, both of which stand as a proud testament to her crew. The remains of the propeller's boss (centre of the propeller), can be seen in the maintenance compound adjacent to where *Britannia* is moored.

In order to convert *Britannia* into a tourist attraction which is accessible to all, bulkheads were moved, and access ways were cut into the sides of the Yacht.

In 2012, *Britannia* was taken into dry-dock for maintenance. Unfortunately, when her mooring lines were released she listed slightly, causing a small intake of water. This was due to her lack of stability which was caused by so many changes and adaptations made on board, such as the addition of the Tea Room located on the Royal Deck. This problem was very soon rectified by adding some ballast which then enabled her to be towed to the dry-dock. The dry-docking went very well, and *Britannia* is not required to visit again until 2030. However, on a yearly basis she undergoes an underwater survey which is carried out by divers to ensure all is in good order.

Kinloch Anderson of Leith (Her Majesty The Queen, Prince Philip and Prince Charles' kiltmakers), supply the tartan uniforms worn by Visitor Assistants and the staff in the Britannia gift shop. It is the corporate tartan of the Britannia Charitable Trust and as such, is not for sale, although you can buy ties and small items designed in this tartan. It is made up of five colours each representing the following parts of *Britannia* - red for below the water line, blue for the ships' sides, Royal Navy blue for the Royal Navy, gold for the 24-carat gold line around the ship and white for the superstructure.

Items on display around *Britannia* are from two collections. The Royal Collection (which now includes the MOD Collection), and the Officer's Wardroom Collection. Additional items on display have been donated by previous serving Yotties, their families or others who have a connection with *Britannia*.

In 2010, top secret Government documents were released which explained how the Royal Yacht *Britannia* would have been used by The Queen in time of war. It was imperative that The Queen was kept safe, as in addition to Her the Prime Minister would be a high priority for attacking, and Her Majesty is the only person with power to appoint a new Prime Minister. The plan formally known as the 'Python System' designated the Royal Yacht as a floating bunker for The Queen. The plans in place saw *Britannia* sailing in the area of the West Coast of Scotland around the many Lochs, thus enabling her to evade Soviet radar. This is one of the reasons why *Britannia's* radio rooms were fitted with the most sophisticated equipment available at the time.

Britannia is on the National Register of Historic Vessels. This register includes ships such as: the *Cutty Sark*, *HMS Victory*, *HMS Belfast*, *HMS Warrior*, the *Mary Rose*, the *Queen Mary* and *SS Great Britain*.

It has been said that if in the mid-1990s the Conservatives and Labour parties had talked to each other in a similar way, to that of Prime Minister Clement Attlee and Opposition Leader Winston Churchill (when they had discussed the prospect of the now present Royal Yacht, following WW2), then perhaps there would have been a new Royal Yacht. Alas, they didn't. Discussions in Parliament have suggested that post Brexit may be the correct time to consider the construction of a new Royal Yacht - *so watch this space!!*

DEFINITIONS

Binnacle - a casing which houses and protects navigational instruments, in particular the ship's compass.

Bulwark – frames the exposed parts of a ship's deck to afford it some protection from the elements

Chronometer - a clock used for accurate time keeping. It is required for accurate navigation and to calculate positions (compass bearing and declination), of stars for morning and evening star sights using a sextant.

Sextant – an instrument used in navigation to obtain accurate angles between objects, e.g. between the horizon and a star or between two lighthouses.

SONAR is an abbreviation of SOund NAvigation and Ranging. This instrument gives the depth of water under the keel.

One **Fathom** is 6 ft.

One **Nautical mile** is 6080 ft (statute mile 5280 ft).

One **Cable** is $^1/_{10}$ of a nautical mile.

One **Nautical League** is 3 nautical miles.

One **Shackle** is 15 fathoms or 90 ft, also known as a Shot of Chain.

BIBLIOGRAPHY/REFERENCES

The following sources have formed an integral part of the research undertaken by the author to aid in the writing of this book.

- Britannia the Official History by Richard Johnstone-Bryden

- Gibraltar Chronicle Archives.

- John Brown Ship Yard.

- Letters from Fish to his Admiral.

- National Historic Ships - www.nationalhistoricships.org.uk

- Naval warships - www.worldnavalships.com/forums/showthread.php?t=10626 (website no longer displays an active forum online at this time).

- Pool Museum Society- https://poolemuseumsociety.wordpress.com/2014/01/09/the-fate-of-the-mistletoe/

- Queen Victoria's Journals – http://www.queenvictoriasjournals.org

- Royal Collection - www.royalcollection.org.uk/collection

- Royal Yacht Britannia - www.royalyachtbritannia.co.uk

- Sailtrain - www.sailtrain.co.uk

- The Gibraltar Garrison Library. - Admiral Lord Nelson Archives.

- The Life Story of a Fish – Captain J.S. Dalglish CVO CBE.

- The Queen's Floating Palace – Brian Hoy.

- TM Utley, St Helens.

- Trinity House – www.trinityhouse.co.uk

- Whitechapel Bell Foundry, London.

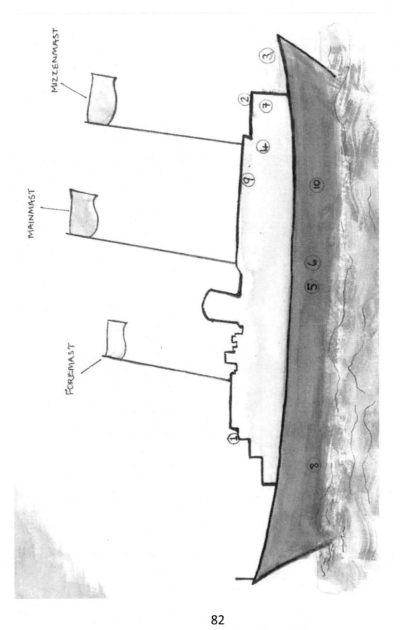

MIZZENMAST

MAINMAST

FOREMAST

1. Royal Bridge

2. Verandah Deck

3. Quarter Deck

4. Grand Staircase

5. Boiler Room

6. Engine Room

7. Drawing Room

8. Crews Accommodation

9. Royal Apartments

10. Household Staff Accommodation